Cello's Tears

Cello's Tears

Geza Tatrallyay
Foreword by Abriana Jetté

ISBN: 194141608X
ISBN 978-1-941416-08-2 paperback
ISBN 978-1-941416-09-9 electronic book
Library of Congress Number: 2015931860

P.R.A. Publishing
P.O. Box 211701
Martinez, GA 30917
www.prapublishing.com

Cover photography and design adapted from a photograph by Andrew Sunderland taken on September 24, 2008

_____

The following poems have been previously published: "A Wanderer's Evensong (After Goethe)," *Quarry*, summer 1983, Volume 32/3; "Dawn Impressions," published as "Dawn Dreams," *American Poetry Anthology*, spring/summer 1983, Volume II, Number 1–2; "Echoes," *Pierian Spring*, autumn 1983; "Autumnal Question," *Quarry*, winter 1984, Volume 33/1.

Printed in the United States

Table of Contents

Dedication

For Sebastian

Acknowledgments

I would like to thank the team at P.R.A. Publishing for making *Cello's Tears* a reality. First, my gratitude goes to Lucinda Clark for seeing merit or perhaps even some beauty in my poetry, and second to Rashida Weedon for her patience and forbearance in working with me to improve the manuscript I first submitted. My thanks also go to Abriana Jetté and to Dusty Sang at Thirsty Media for all their positive encouragement and recognition.

Foreword

The Greek word *poeima*, from which we derive the English word poem, literally translates into "something made" or "workmanship." Poetry is hard work. It is the effort of creation and art and emotion forced into stanzas. It is at once nonfiction and fiction—equal parts song and written word. It is the manifestation of what Geza Tatrallyay refers to as "emotional meaning...in a unique world." It is all about us, and *Cello's Tears*, Tatrallyay's first collection of poetry, serves as the bridge that connects cultures with language.

Though it might seem reasonable for there to exist some sort of disconnect in a poem that relies on two languages, it is actually true that bilingual students, readers, and speakers are more apt to empathize with those around them than one who only understand his or her native tongue. The beauty of living with two or more languages is, of course, that one may live in two (or more) worlds and observe the most mundane of happenstances from various perspectives. The poems in this collection resonate with cultural sentimentality and lyrical piquancy.

Tatrallyay's vision is to redefine emotional boundaries for the contemporary world while reflecting on his past. His brain exists in two spaces; our speaker thinks in multiple languages. To represent these emotions accurately, Tatrallyay cuts back, offering sharp, terse phrasing. For instance, in "Autumnal Question," summer and fall are void of color; still, the simple truth speaks to readers through the unsaid knowledge of what always follows fall: winter. Death. Like an unfinished prayer, the fragmentary, mostly monosyllabic syntax of such poems immediately arrests readers' senses. In this way, reader and speaker dance along the blurred lines of reality and memory, shifting from country to country and from season to season.

In "Autumnal Question II," a poem in which earthly matters are personified as agents of the afterlife, the speaker wonders "what clouds there, all dressed in black," and this haunts him. Tatrallyay's work describes a death that readers are comfortable imagining, a death we fear and attempt, though in vain, to avoid. This interplay between the living and the nonliving, and between languages, coerces readers into thinking about individual failings while simultaneously guiding them to a deeper appreciation of their surroundings. Thus creeps up the unavoidable and ultimate question, the heart of *Cello's Tears*: the speaker's craving to know what comes after our time in the physical world.

Visually and verbally, Tatrallyay propels the movement of the collection backward and forward, creating an immeasurable capacity to each poem's shape. In their confessional tone, the poems transform into philosophical meditations on the human condition. They are emotional ramifications for a soul deeply altered by the world around him. They are observant, finely tuned recordings of thought, of time, and of history.

It is hard work to create a collection with breadth and depth, one that touches readers on multiple levels; it is even more difficult to put together a collection that is accessible for readers from multiple cultures. Geza Tatrallyay has done this work. He has crafted a world of language and symbol, of haunting figures and sentimental lyricism, and in observing and painstakingly articulating the aches and joys of human experience, *Cello's Tears* is an immediately thought-provoking and soul-satisfying collection.

Here are poems you'll want to return to. Here is *Cello's Tears*.

—Abriana Jetté

Introduction

I wrote the poems in this collection over quite a few years and in the many countries where I have lived. The influences therefore are varied insofar as they derive from the different cultural, linguistic, and natural contexts.

Thus, when I lived in Japan, I experimented with the sparse rigor of expressing a feeling in the seventeen *on* (or syllables) of the haiku and the five units and thirty-one *on* of the tanka. Japan also spawned the poems "Japanese Feeling" and "Japanese Feeling II." Montreal, Quebec, is clearly the birthplace of "Jogging on Golgotha," while bucolic Vermont gave rise to "The Cemetery," "Frogs in the Pond," "Evening: Heron and Pond," and "Squirrel," among others.

The one common thread in the collection is the exploration of poetry as translation. In the first instance, poems can be seen as the translation or the encoding of raw emotion into words. I then go beyond this and, in some of my work, explore translation from one language to another, which involves the decoding of what is written in one language to get at the feeling behind the words in the poem and then re-encoding that into words in the second language. Examples of this are "A Wanderer's Evensong (After Goethe)," the lovely little poem written in German by Johann Wolfgang von Goethe; my own "Autumnal Question," first written in Hungarian and then translated to English; and the enigmatic French Canadian poet Émile Nelligan's "Vieux Piano," or "Old Piano."

It is but a short step from translating works between languages to trying to translate the feeling encapsulated in another art form into poetry. Many of the poems in this collection are such attempts to re-encode in words the emotional meaning or existential angst or unique world view—always very personal—behind works of music ("Death Strikes Up...," "On Hearing Mahler Once Again," "Valse Triste et Sentimentale"); painting ("Tableau: Last Judgment Revisited," "Fragment: Reaching," "Distant Searchlights...," "Query"); and sculpture ("Creation").

In some works, I experiment with language. Thus, the poems "Fragment from a Dying Civilization," "Imbroglio," "On Propaganda," and "Warning" deconstruct words to enhance the message, pictorially or otherwise, while in others, unconventional word use attempts to do the same.

Finally, since poetry is verbal music, I have organized the collection into four parts, much as the symphonic form has four movements. Parts II and III comprehend the works influenced by music and the visual arts, respectively. The collection ends with "Dollops of Drivel," which tries to convey the Wittgensteinian frustration with the inherent impossibility of communicating the fullness of one's feelings. Enjoy.

—Geza Tatrallyay

1. Teardrops

Echoes

The distilled soul's silent song
yearns to break out, to penetrate
the evening's thickening mist
toward the distant lightning
where shadows play momentous games:

my song remains an intention—
it cannot escape this deep well.

Oh, these echoes reverberate
sonorously, like cello's tears
streaming among silhouettes
in this useless melancholy.

Japanese Feeling

By the dim candlelight
I await your coming
with love and soft music:

I hear only the wind
walk softly down the path
that snowflakes now cover—
frozen tears the world wept,
feeling my loneliness.

Japanese Feeling II

By the fire's glow,
among the shadows,
I sit, unmoving:

outside, in the dark,
elements battle,
while within my soul,
too, in harmony,
a wild storm rages.

Tanka: Fingertips

the plum tree's naked
fingertips stroke my sadness:

if only they were
your fingertips, your soft touch,

and the blossoms bloomed again...

Fragment: Nostalgia

We stride against the tide of time
to commune with phantom fantasies
from the shifting dunes of the past,
an ozone pure childhood in the clouds

Lacrimae Mundi

Clandestine shadows tiptoe across the silence
fearful of the hot anger of the noonday sun
god whose dazzling gaze tames even the ocean's waves
or those of the mind-consuming thought and passion
and who blinds all who would defy the promenade
from darkness to darkness across a barren sky

tortured trees dare not whisper ancient secrets
first dreamt in the terror of childhood by moonlight
and sanctified by years of communion with earth
in that infinite nighttime while the tyrant slept

scorching hot rays petrify all liquid freedom
vaporize the soul and deflate our wildest hopes
to the boring mechanical tick of some clock
whose deafening fanfare faithfully glorifies
an eternal emergence beyond our inkling
and hammers frustration and those repressed fears
into a devastating monstrous certitude

fate of child death and cremation rushed ungently
by an orb's unwavering march across the sky
that morning dreamt rosebud of love weeps frozen tears
for a lost world the sun would never tolerate.

Haiku: Solitude and Space

Sobs of solitude:
I do not hear an
echo from infinite space.

Dawn Impressions

Morning tears
on the meadow,
in my eye—

for this magic
day's dawning,
the nascent light,
this beauty
that cannot last:
a victim
of time's outrage.

Warning

war
ning:
war
will
wage

On My Mother's Death

(Her name was Lily)

Only raw pain and tears,
a lonesome emptiness,
linger to desecrate
deified memories
of untouchable love,
a mother's selflessness.

Suffering orphans now,
we curse a perverse god
who dared crush the perfect
lily that was your life.

Statement of Irrelevance

For those who believed
and died unknowing,
the moment emerging
feels no compassion:
they are irrelevant
to life unfolding.

Fragments of a Mood

I

Autumn has blown into my eyes,
and through the double haze of tears
I see dead and browned leaves falling—
aimless specks of reality
slowly floating this way and that
while eternity passes by.

II

Now I feel the oppressiveness
of the wind still, when nothing moves
and nothing lives, except the heat
and the sweat sitting on my brow,
collecting like pus in a wound
infected years, eons ago.

III

...

Seaside Fragment

Quiet dreams the soul by the sea,
lulled into another sphere
by the reeling stare of the stars
and the wonder of the water;
time is lost among grains of sand,
and the world is washed away:
laughing waves lap on the shores
of yesterday's misty memory
where children toiled aimlessly
to build fairy castles of sand,
where paper boats of hopes and loves
challenged the stormy ocean...

Fragment of a Moonlit Evening

A misty, translucent peace
drops onto this darkening world
where the sky is washed-out gray,
the land, a sleeping silhouette...

Myriads of crickets chirp,
frightened, aimless in the black night;
now and again, some toad croaks—
they all decay, unheard, unsung...

Only the moon, so distant,
asserts itself, illuminates
that unfathomable fog
between my soul and nothingness...

Fragment from a Dying Civilization

con

flag

rat

ion

creeps

around

the corner

consuming

all

con...

Fragment, in Flight, at Sunset

Below me,
glacier clouds
mellow
in a disappearing orange sea
that flows from the sun
toward the all-consuming
purple-gray haze of evening:

the celestial drama
draws,
once again,
to a perfect,
measured close.

And I,
who slump here
like a weakened coil
among these colors,
this movement,
wonder at my pitiful role
and weep
in fear
of a disillusioned destiny.

Night Presence

rainsteps on the rooftop
rouse me to the terror
of your absent presence
that lingers all around:

an unwashable stain
preempting sanity,
ordering my universe;

your warmth has not yet cooled,
stray strands of your hair still
tickle against my skin,
and your elfin voice
speaks at me from the dark:

the face of the night world
masks your present absence;
I drift in your teardrops
back to oblivion.

II. Concerto

A Wanderer's Evensong

(After Goethe)

Above the peaks
A peace hovers:
In the treetops,
Hardly a breeze.
The birds are quiet in the woods—
Wait my friend: soon
You too shall rest.

Haiku (Two Variations on a Fall Theme)

We sing summer's song,
not heeding the falling leaves
that augur autumn.

We sing summer's song,
not heeding the morning frost
that colors the leaves.

Death Strikes Up

(Hommage à Mahler)

Death strikes up its mocking laughter,
madly jeers at life's symphony—
the tragic, daring song of earth.

Seeing life, the monster rises,
raises its eerie serpent head,
and in spite of the day's glory,
invades the sun's perfect garden,
dancing to the ballet of time,
leaping from flower to flower
in an orgy of destruction.

Prometheus

I kept wake with you by the sea,
held you through the fearful long night;
together we lived that dream
of the lullaby by the waves,
crystal of love's moody guitar.

Together we watched dark bear light,
the heavens blush orange and gold;
we beheld the birth of the sun,
whose magic wand would wake the world
from its primordial slumber.

I felt the chemistry of life
swell with pride in your loving womb;
I was proto-life in the sea,
an amphibian emerging
to the hazardous atmosphere.

With you I was maker of all,
creator of our universe,
of beauty and goodness and truth:
from the smoldering lava cliffs,
I hurled forth the Titan's challenge.

II

Years coasted by; now I am old.
Eagles have gouged out my eyes;
you merged into the awful night,
and I, the cripple, roam alone
these desolate ruins of our world.

I can feel our sun grow colder
as evening's veil drops onto earth;
spring shall never blossom again.
I hear only the night music,
finale to life's symphony.

Yet I still clamber to the crags
by our primeval sea of fire,
and in a quivering voice
roar above the eternal storm
my Titan's taunt: I am a man!

The eyes of my failing mind weep
with your joy at the birth of all;
my memories of our short wake
are timeless, indestructible:
the abyss echoes my challenge.

Dirge

The threatening storm's thundering dirge
dyes the face of this frivolous world
with solemn and ominous shadows
that shout an unremembered terror
to those who stop to sense their rhythm—
a berserk world that unheeds itself
and whirls, cackling, in its dung, toward
an orgasmic leap into the void.

Soliloquy

I

Undreamt dreams
germing in the mind

like a child accident
the unconceived fruit
of conception

a time-lapse of life
unfolds from the seed

with a monster ferocity
an organic splendor

the lion trainer lashes out
and fancy somersaults
unexpected

into the eyes
of the bewildered spectator

II

I
walk
naked
down a craggy footpath
inside this azure-blue bubble
ice pick poised
blinded by the savage blizzard

I walk
in an unknown when
through an unknown where

and in this bewitched twilight
I can just eye
forests of frosted firs
frolicking with frozen corpses

celebrating victory
over Macbeth

III

Eons stray in seconds
and I
into an arid land
a desert
where demons dance

round and round
a maypole mirage
of pigtails and petticoats

cacti attack
mischievously

my battered
bloody body
is deserted
to a merciless
frigid sun
that imagines itself
god
among kneeling grains of sand

(I will not sing a psalm
nor speak an ode
except in praise
of my suffering kind)

IV

The desert
passes
while I
stand still
in a silent,
sad universe
and all
all is blind mist

I feel
tridents
in the paws
of invisible ghouls
prick my soul
tapping
the warm wine blood
of life

and does this cold dampness
masticate my marrow
in vengeance
for Adam's folly

V

Some inexorable vision
walks before me
drags me behind

a relic
from those childhood illusions

gnawed to atoms
by the rats and insects
of life's delusions

I lurch on
a soliloquy
in empty space.

On Hearing Mahler Once Again

Above the moonlit lake,
I hover
among silvered clouds:

Far below,
in the waves,
distorted faces
seem to scream
in panic,
and they drown,
disgusting.

I hear only the wind
and the slender moonshine
dance passionately
to Mahler's genius.

And the stars
chide me
so lovingly

(like grandparents a child)
for this innocent,
glorious pride.

I escape
to a separate,
a rarer realm,

above shimmering peaks,
beyond morsels of time.

I empty
into a bottomless universe;
neither skin
nor cellular membrane,
neither dams
nor mountains
can bind me.

Opposites collapse:
ecstasy
becomes melancholy
(and vice versa);
everything
and nothing
defy definition.

Far below,
a perfected nature
whirls sensually
in a sublime reading:

I feel
a vacuum
suck the molecules
of my soul,
and my mind
merges
with nothingness.

Only the music is.

On Propaganda

Slo
guns

can
can

kill
too

Softly the Tallow Glows

Softly the tallow glows,
casting shadows that sault
and dance across the walls.

Love, let there be no wind,
no puff to extinguish
the flame of your passion.

For then I, a shadow
cast by your soul, would merge
into the creeping night.

Valse Triste et Sentimentale

(Hommage á Maurice Ravel)

I

Two souls dance:
valse triste et
sentimentale,

floating waltz,
among clouds,
across the sky;

two souls fly
in splendid
three-quarter time,

floating waltz
inside clouds
of perfect sighs.

II

Echoes of death
sneak, unnoticed,
bar by black bar,
along the song,
till they usurp
the melody:

death himself
leads our souls
in a crazed crescendo
toward an unending
climax of silence.

Viscosity

this viscous wistful dream
backward jogs to nullity
a faint sonata sings
from what past inside the sea
where nothing still exists
(except a premonition
that may not come to pass)
and fogs forward playing life
graycloudwalls imprison
the logical searching light
reflect and focus same
like a magnifying glass
gleefully incending
this insipid soul of straw

Lullaby

We wake to waves
softly stroking
the sizzling sand
where we once loved:

an eternal
lullaby that
drowns out our love
and buries it
among infinite grains of sand.

Moments Musicaux
(Music and Physics)

Moments musicaux
float in the night ether:
tone and time spiral,
substance and form recede
inexorably
into infinity
toward the black hole
of thermodynamic
annihilation,
of everlasting death.

Haiku (Two Variations on a Spring Theme)

I

(In a Western mode)

When spring's madrigal
sighs over the world,
ecstasy stirs souls to dance.

II

(In an Eastern mode)

When spring's silken sigh
strums the world's koto,
joy stirs nature's soul to dance.

Old Piano

(After Émile Nelligan, 1897)
The soul in this old instrument no longer sighs:
what a somber mien its lowered cover imparts;
thrown out from the salon, it naps in the shadows,
this ancient misanthrope soured by solitude.

I still recall the innumerable nocturnes
my mother used to play me, and weeping, I dream
of those evenings, long since passed to the penumbra,
when Liszt was called triste and Beethoven the end.

Piano of ebony, symbol of my life:
my poor soul, like yours, is ravished of happiness;
you lack an artist, and I the true ideal.

And still you sleep there, my sole joy in the world:
who then shall bring your funereal keyboard back
to life with triumphant song, oh profound distress?

Haiku, in a Western Mode

Mozart, books and booze
lubricate the mind's journey
through this hellish maze.

Haiku: Evening Sigh

In the evening calm
was it your sigh that
made the dying leaves flutter?

Wind and Cello

The wind sighs
through the poplars' leaves:
the bow that makes
the cello's strings sing

III. Pictures at an Exhibition

Tableau: Last Judgment Revisited

(Hommage á Michelangelo Buonarroti)

I

Waters are tumbling
over the cliffside
dropping to the cold
blackness of the shade
millions of miles
below
where nothing moves
where nothing lives.

The deafening roar
of the waterfall
fades in the silence
of the gorge below
as even the birds
above
try to escape
from the landscape.

The continuum
of all light and dark
of color and black
begins in the sky
and ends in the gorge
below
where silence rains
and silence reigns.

II

Angels try to fly
or creep to escape
the suck of Scylla
first the wings break off
then bodies tumble
below
where good is not
and god is naught.

Some try to hold on
to a root or crag
to climb up the cliff
to the top again
where they saw some light
above
but no success
and no redress.

So gradually
cell by living cell
blood drop by blood drop
the body crumbles
screams into the void
below
where nothing breeds
and darkness feeds.

III

The brain that perceives
the painful painting
the fallen falling
tenses in terror
while corpses pile up
below
it just crumbles
it too tumbles.

The elastic soul
hanging from a branch
tears with a loud scream
and plummets below
while the wanton whine
above
choosing their urn
waiting their turn.

The painter cannot
alter his tableau
though he hears the roar
of the falling tears
echo from the crags
below
the sacrifice
that his son dies.

Fragment: Reaching

... arms reaching
like adam and father,
like stalagmite
and stalactite...

fingertips,
yearning
to touch
across
an infinite
emptiness...

Haiku: Image of Blood

The snow in the field
turned crimson when I looked down
from our high tower.

Haiku: Self-Vision

My mind is a cloud,
ambling aimlessly among
the pines on the peaks.

Haiku: High

Flying high, we dip
into dark clouds, through which souls
pass the other way.

Venous Leaves

dry
brittle
venous
leaves
float
in the wind
of death:
I am afraid

Haiku: Fossil Shells

Fossil shells in stone
remind me: the sea stood here
once, where I now stand.

Haiku: Slopes and Abyss

Steep slopes climb
to a meaningless summit,
drop to the abysmal void.

Haiku: Wrinkles

The waveless water
mirrors wrinkles wrought
by the voyage of the sun.

Haiku: Crimson Glaciers

Crimson glaciers ooze
within this wintry being
freezing thought, feeling.

Haiku: Fresh Snow

A
crystal
of fresh snow
clings
to your hair
like
I
in my dreams
to you

Creation

(Hommage à Henry Moore)
Bang,
and the brain
bursts,
explodes—
incandescent white;
headless, limbless
feminine forms
float unfettered
in the morass
of creation:
life
art
unfolding.

Wintry Winds

wintry winds steal
summer's glow

white sheets of snow
shroud earth's smile

while I only die

Étude of Light and Dark
(Advent of Twilight)

A lambent light clings to the land
and trembles still among the trees
remembering love's ecstasy

Deep in the wrinkles of the earth
twilight shadows merge their forces
to march against life's gay luster

Lucifer rapes the light my love
and burns the world a charcoal black
banishing the touch of softness
from that which was the firmament.

You Are Dying Now, Father Winter

I

You are dying now, father winter,
melting into rivulets of new life:
where winter's icy will ruled the world,
only a languid memory remains.

We leaf back through silent, solo times
in pursuit of a seductive semblance
fleeing from us among frozen forms
in the shadows of a sleepy forest.

Or gaze, snow-blind, from atop this knoll,
backward across the widening crevasse
at a white wisp of lingering smoke
inviting the mind to a fireside chat.

II

For some time yet, we shall remember
this notch on the staff of our passing years
and mourn the parting of the sculptor
who molded the shape of this moving now.

But the light of the dark of your death
is this fresh joy that pervades the spirit
of all who see the flowers budding
and listen to the nightingale's singing.

I feel the sun coax expectations
of some new and untried combinations
from those tired and worn, aged forms:
eagerly, I flow to the next moment.

Haiku: Sun Glitter

sun glitter shimmers
on the mirror of the pond:
clouds threaten, like death

Hoarfrost

Crystalline
fronds of hoar
etch the pane,
refracting
the morning's
first stray rays
that venture
to enter
this dank space—

but day dawns, like love: rays
fructify, and the warmth,
the warmth of the sun's smile
pierces the wintry crust,
irradiating it,
consuming its cancer,
and bestowing the glow
of life once again
on a dark and dead room—

my soul.

Haiku: Winter's Whiteness

winter's whiteness now
cloaks the grass we once loved on
in this quiet glade

Distant Searchlights

(Hommage à Jeremy Smith)
distant searchlights grope through organic clouds:

nervous fingers, seeking to penetrate
that heaving mass of voluptuous flesh;
rays reach out, wanting contact, a response—

while you and I, mere sawed-off stumps, sterile
and separate, cannot bridge the abyss.

Lavender Sky, the Earth Below

lavender sky, the earth below,
etched in a burning orange,
where our father, the sun, has died—

a somber universe explodes
in mauve and pink, lapis above—
another day's execution

a sliver moon, the silver stars
light the meandering mind's way
through the expanding gloom of space

twilight thoughts, deep and dejected
usurp my neural synapses

oh, how dark the night has become!

Time and Solitude

Days, eons stream by,
etching canyons
of melancholy
on a plastic face:

vacant loneliness
pervades the being
and settles, like dust,
on this fragile veil.

Laser beams of time
and solitude sear
the fetus in its
unpierceable womb:
we know only its
faint, pallid death mask.

Fragment, with Clouds

I
fly
high
above
a soft sea
of sensible clouds

that shield
my dreams of love,
my heroic fantasies

from shattering
in that mirror of reality...

Frogs in the Pond

in the late spring gelatinous frog spawn
floats in the pond: undulating streamers
of eggs extruded by the female frog

Marcia, my wife, attacks them with a rake
pulling them out to dry in the hot sun
against my son's and my loud objections

but she gives up: the task is too daunting
and she will not defeat evolution;
many escape and stay to the next stage

a few weeks go by and in the water
myriads of tadpoles swim and frolic
among the one or two occasional humans

the next time we come there is breaking news:
a royal family of handsome frogs
inhabits the rocks and mud by the pond
hunting flies, mosquitoes and other vermin

metamorphosis has transpired: herbivore
has become carnivore; prey is now predator

I skim the surface swimming lazily
and see four pairs of frog eyes watching me
carefully from under their rocky ledge,
gold dusted eyebrows crowning emerald
green bodies: king, queen, prince and princess frog

Autumn Has Perched on the Gable Sill

Autumn has perched on the gable sill,
refractory, like the hooded Reaper,
demanding entry, forbidding escape:

the pane filters the dying summer light,
splays its spectral hues, like a peacock's tail,
across this veined, wizened face: I sit still,
unblinking, while the image of the scythe
reflects from glassy eyes, hacks at the flesh...

The Cemetery

The Methodist cemetery on the North Road
has tombstones dating back to eighteen hundred ten:
Jack Rousseau, Francis Dubois, Ralph Rhoades, Ted
Campbell,
the dead long departed into oblivion

Its mossy graves are cracked or have corners missing,
like those ancient books found in an antiquary,
names and dates and epitaphs scarcely legible,
the acid etching erased by wind and weather

Only a few new tombs in shiny gray marble,
grave monuments to those whose extinction still pains
their still-living friends, are graced by the stars and
stripes
or drying bouquets, blown-out candles, yellow ribbons

In the summer, the grass between the tombs is mowed
by a fat woman wearing shorts on a tractor,
lovingly clipped around the stones by her husband:
they too will soon lie there fertilizing the lawn

In the winter, lined in battle formation,
only the headstones of the bravest dare to raise
their white-shakoed pates above the frozen snow line
to see the living pass through this forbidding world
Year in, year out, relentlessly, eternally

The cemetery gives
only temporal stay
to mortality as
death defeats all,
save time

Fragment: Something and Nothing

Stars are shining tonight
silver specks of something
in this senseless nothing
of finite loneliness

We fill the emptiness
with an imagined world
and cling to feigned feelings
to feed the fragile mind...

Evening: Heron and Pond

dusk silence

a gray heron
skates gracefully
over the pond
    a blade slicing
    the oil fleck
    shimmering through
    tarry forest greens

a violent flutter
of pterodactyl wings
the bird evolves
into a receding
silhouette against
a polyphonic sky
    vermilion
    and indigo
    aquamarine
    and burnt orange

and vanishes

as the sun bleeds to death

IV. Unanswered Questions

Epigram

You ask: why am I?
And I: why the why?

Epigram II

Rock that stands there by and by,
how much longer will you live than I?

Haiku, with Daisies

Why are those daisies
I brought for you yesterday
all brown and wilted?

Graying

I
look
for a peg
to hang my life upon
but in the graying wall
I can find

Autumnal Question

(translated from original written in Hungarian)

Fall has come;

summer flees.

Under the redding oak tree,

what lurks for me?

Autumnal Question II

What clouds there, all dressed in black:
solemn pallbearers marching
to a funereal rhythm—
this dying heartbeat of life,
this pounding silence that sounds
as summer's softness passes.

Yet those trees there, on the shore,
crowding, teeming, so alive,
frocked in happy colors—
could they just be ghouls in guise,
mocking this advanced season
and rejoicing at life's death?

That pink on the horizon,
and that lapis-blue above,
those chameleon colors—
golds and greens and oranges—
are they just the fireworks
that mark the end of all life?

Autumnal Question III

From this crag
I see a sky
rusting with age,
like leaves that fall,
decay to dust;

I wonder: do
the setting sky,
the rotting leaves—
can they perceive
that I too am
being ended?

Autumnal Question IV

Love has fallen like dry leaves
from the tree of our life:
I stand alone and naked
to winter's icy wind;
alone and naked I stand
in a skeleton world.
But is that not you I see
on the river's far side—
you, a sapling pine, mingling
again with lusting trees
in this flowering forest
of life that must go on?

Seaward Blows the Wind

Seaward blows the wind
toward dark and cold
where there are no stars.

Ghostly waves awake
and die shivering
out there in the night.

The somber sky weeps
with tragic fury
or mocking laughter.

A lonely seagull
screeches in the gale:
the vulture of hope.

Frantic in the dusk,
my mind is flooded
with aching questions
that bear no answers.

Lackluster Days

lackluster days
loiter
in this mire
of middlingness:
can there be
no escape
save dreams and death?

Drooping Skies

drooping skies
a wetted fen

I wander
  and wonder

will winter's love
come back again?

Thoughtful Question

When these thoughts have ended,
there might be no time:

no time for a kiss,
an embrace,
or a smile,
or for that matter,
that one telling glance...

Will you then,
when the darkness comes,
remember me
by these, my thoughts?

Imbroglio

In
what
in
fer
nal
im
bro
glio

will
end
this
cos
mic
sce
nar
i
o
?

Jogging on Golgotha

The skies wept when I went jogging today
up by de Maisonneuve's skeleton cross
on Mount Royal (or was it Golgotha?)...

out my house, along cement streets, empty
with concocted life, up crumbling stairs...

I do not hesitate at traffic lights
and cut, unblinking, through at least two cars,
leaving their speechless occupants speechless...

(Have you, friend, seen this anthill, Golgotha?)

easily I transcend the mortal realm
of men and machine and their hateful words...

(Where is this Golgotha, friend, if not here?)

I scramble up a lonely, rutted path,
surprised that even those snakes of water
(or of blood, friend?) slither the other way...

and voodoo eyes of spectator trees dare
to glare from the darkness, assembled there
to mock my tortured, senseless ascension...

(How many men must have died and decayed
to dust, my friend, to make this Golgotha?)

scourge-like branches lash my naked flesh,
and those sharpened thorns shred my face and scalp...

(Why all this pain, all this suffering, friend,
on this ever-higher hill, Golgotha?)

on bleeding hands and knees I reach the cross,
raise bony, mangled arms toward the sky
in purported gratitude, learned by rote,
praying to pry open the golden gates
of a graceful heaven that should welcome
me to retire into eternity...

but my trembling hands slice, knifelike, only
through a ceiling of tempestuous clouds,
releasing a vengeful torrent of rain
that washes me away to nothingness...

Prayers

prophylactic prayers float
through an empty universe
in search of a sterile god,
a utopian heaven:

only the sinister void's
silence echoes in reply.

Squirrel

That rustling sound from under the brown
blanket that covers our black earth—

Is it a squirrel scurrying
to find that last morsel before
cold and white bleach the living world?

The Changeling Hour

silhouettes of barren branches
reach for heaven's last light
and maul the pastel peace
of twilight's misting shroud...

oh, that changeling hour
when phantom hares
scurry to elude those
galloping hooves from hell...

and I, a thinking man,
ponder in vain
the meaning
of this passing...

Mist o'er a Marsh

mist o'er a marsh
    hanging
    hanging

lost among reeds

    muffled grayness
    brackish oozing
    frozen marrow

where to go
where to go
where

Savor the Night

savor the night:
    soporific
    darkness descends,
    annihilates
    the conscious mind,
    swaddles the soul;

savor the night:
    while ego rests,
    libido speeds,
    raging, through dreams,
    worlds, well beyond
    the common ken;

savor the night:
    your naked self,
    luscious, splendid,
    spread beside me,
    and I, lusting
    to violate
    every pore;

am I fated
only to dream?

Query

(Hommage à J. M. W. Turner)
The sun is god:
is there a God?

Dollops of Drivel

what dollops of drivel drain from within
where those momentous feelings rise and fall
like lost corks on the choppy waves of life

why are there no words to convey the raw
and burning beauty of this energy
bursting inside my heart, my mind, my soul?